Contents

Eat right

Eating the right food is really important for keeping you happy and healthy, and helping your body to grow strong. But what is the 'right' food? It's all about making sure you have a balanced diet.

A balanced diet

Eating a balanced diet means eating the right mix of different foods. To help you do this, all foods can be put into one of five groups. You should try to eat some foods from each of the five groups every day.

The fantastic five

- Milk and diary foods – foods such as cream, cheese, yoghurt and milk are all in this group.

- Bread, other cereals and potatoes – this group includes foods such as oats, rice, pasta and breakfast cereals.

- Fruit and vegetables – fresh, frozen and canned fruit and veg are all in this group, as are 100 per cent fruit or vegetable juices.

- Foods that contain fats or sugars – this group includes butter, oil, cakes, sweets and mayonnaise.

- Meat, fish and alternatives – all meat, fish and seafood are in this group, as well as **protein**-packed meat alternatives such as eggs, nuts and tofu.

Ve ... es

Honor Head

QED Publishing

QED

First published in the UK in 2006 by
QED Publishing
A Quarto Group company
226 City Road
London EC1V 2TT
www.qed-publishing.co.uk

A catalogue record for this book is available from the British Library.

ISBN 1 84538 480 6

Written by Honor Head
Designed by Danny Pyne
Edited by Hannah Ray and Barbara Bourassa
Consultancy by Roy Balam and Sarah Schenker of the British Nutrition Foundation
Photographer Michael Wicks
Illustrations by Bill Greenhead

Publisher Steve Evans
Art Director Zeta Davies
Editorial Director Jean Coppendale

Printed and bound in China

Picture credits

Key: t = top, b = bottom, c = centre, l = left, r = right, FC = front cover

Alamy/Geoff du Feu FC; **Corbis**/Sharie Kennedy 7cl /photocuisine 26tr
/Envision 26cl /photocuisine 27tl /Philip Gould 27cl; **Getty**/Stockfood
Creative, Quentin Bacon 26br /Stockfood Creative, Harry Bischof 27br.

Before undertaking any activity which involves eating or the preparation of food,
always check whether the children in your care have any food allergies. In a
classroom situation, prior written permission from parents may be required.

Words in **bold** can be found in the glossary on page 30.

Think in thirds

This diagram shows a plate divided up into the five groups. For a really great diet, try to make sure that one-third of what you eat is made up of fruit and vegetables, one-third is made up of bread, cereals and potatoes, and the last third is made up of a mix of dairy foods, meat, fish and alternatives, and foods that contain fats and sugars.

Weblink

Some countries, such as the USA and Australia, use a special food pyramid to help explain how to eat a healthy and balanced diet. To find out more, visit www.mypyramid.gov/kids

Why eat a balanced diet?

No one food can provide all the **nutrients** your body needs to grow properly, to fight off illness and to give you enough energy to get through the day. That's why it's important to eat food from all the groups – to make sure you're giving your body everything it needs.

What are vegetables?

This book is all about vegetables, from the fruit and vegetables group. Vegetables come in all shapes, sizes and colours. They are a very important part of a balanced and healthy diet, so try to eat some for lunch and dinner every day.

Meet the veggies

There are so many different types of vegetables that they are divided into groups. Root vegetables are those, such as carrots and parsnips, whose roots are the part that we actually eat. Each plant grows small green leaves above ground, but the vegetable itself stays underground. Other groups of vegetables include tubers (the potato family), leaves (vegetables such as lettuce), stems (such as asparagus), flowers (for example, cauliflower) and seeds (vegetables such as pumpkins).

Taking the pulse

Beans and lentils are both types of **pulse**. They are not actually a type of vegetable because they are the seeds of certain plants. Pulses are available dried in bags or ready cooked in cans.

Borlotti beans
in sugared salt water

Science bit

Vegetables provide loads of **vitamins** and **minerals** to keep us healthy. They also contain **fibre**, which is essential for our digestive system and helps us to go to the toilet every day. Pulses contain loads of protein, which is especially useful if you are a **vegetarian** or don't eat much meat. Eating a wide range of vegetables and pulses will help you concentrate on your schoolwork and make sure you stay fit, healthy and raring to go.

Try five

Food experts recommend that we eat at least five **portions** of fruit and vegetables every day. For school snacks you could have pieces of raw carrot or celery sticks, and for lunch you could tuck into a bean salad or a **Greek salad**. You could then enjoy some cooked veggies with your evening meal. Five portions? It's easy!

Q. When is a vegetable not a vegetable?
A. When it's a fruit!

Some foods, such as tomatoes, avocados and cucumbers, are actually fruits because they contain seeds. However, they still appear in this book because we eat them as vegetables.

Lunch Choice

Sticks and dips

Grab a veggie stick, scoop up some tasty dip and eat! Vegetable sticks with dips are a fun way towards achieving your recommended five portions of fruits and vegetables a day.

Banana

Yoghurt

Tomato salsa

Bag your batons

You can prepare some sliced vegetables the night before and keep them in the fridge overnight. Ask an adult to slice the veggies into chunky sticks, or batons, and put them into a plastic bag or tub to keep them fresh until lunchtime. Here are some ideal veggies to dip:

Carrots

Baby corn

Cucumber

Green and red pepper

Big dipper

You've got your sticks, now you need your dips. Make tasty and healthy dips from avocados or cottage cheese and chives. Or buy a tray of dips, ready-made **houmous** or **salsa** and add your own crunchy veggie sticks.

Onion and garlic

Cheese and chive

Sour cream and chive

Fruit juice

Thousand Island

Veggie dippers

Houmous

Try it!

Deep-fried vegetables, such as Japanese vegetable tempura, should only be eaten as a once-in-a-while treat.

Fancy a change?

For really grown-up vegetable sticks, try raw cauliflower and broccoli **florets**. They are really tasty and bursting with vitamins. Go on, give them a try!

Call this a vegetable?

When you visit your supermarket you will see lots of different vegetables on sale.

Unsquashable squashes

The vegetables on the right all belong to the squash family. However, they are not really squashy at all as most have a very thick and tough outer skin. When the spaghetti squash is cooked and sliced open, the insides fall out like strands of spaghetti.

Pumpkin

Butternut squash

Spaghetti squash

Courgette

Pak choi

Tropical veg

These vegetables come mainly from very hot places such as Africa, the Caribbean, China, India and Thailand.

Yam

Sweet potato

Okra

Mangetout

Beansprouts

Sugersnap peas

Got mush room?

Mushrooms belong to the **fungi** family. There are many different types of mushroom. Here are just some that you might see in the supermarket:

Portobello – yummy cooked for breakfast.

Button – great eaten raw with dips or sliced in salads.

Chestnut – this is a small portobello.

Shiitake – these have a meaty flavour and are used in Japanese cooking.

Morel – expensive mushrooms that can be used in all sorts of cooking.

Oyster – tasty mushrooms used in Chinese stir-fries.

Chanterelle – this mushroom comes from France.

Winter warmers

Here are some vegetables that you might eat in a hearty stew on a cold winter's day:

Carrots

Parsnips

Leeks

Potatoes

Onion

Turnip

11

Lunch Choice

Winter salad

Mix a pile of chopped vegetables with some mayonnaise for a super-fit lunch. Add a dollop of **horseradish** or mustard for flavour and tuck in at lunchtime.

Apple

Boiled egg

Winter salad

Crunch bunch

When vegetables are cooked they lose some of their vitamins, so it is best to eat a variety of both raw and cooked veggies. A crunchy veggie salad is a tasty way to eat some raw vegetables. Mix cauliflower and broccoli florets, diced carrots, sweetcorn, some diced green or red peppers and sliced celery with low-fat mayonnaise. Add a few herbs and some pepper for taste, and you have a fantastic lunchbox salad that will see you through an afternoon of maths and maybe even science!

WARNING! Make sure that the veg you pick for your crunchy salad are okay to eat raw. Don't try and tuck into a raw potato – you'll end up with a terrible tummy ache!

Noisy but nice

For an ultra-noisy lunch, make some crunchy coleslaw. This is a mixture of sliced white cabbage and grated carrots mixed with low-fat mayonnaise. Try throwing in a few raisins, too. You could even add a chopped apple. It saves having to eat it for pudding afterwards!

Bottle of water

Yoghurt

CHECK IT OUT!

Always eat low-fat mayonnaise if you can. It's better for you.

Dress it up

As an alternative, try a salad with an oil-based dressing. Experiment with a few recipes including olive oil, vinegar and lemon juice. If you make a dressing like this, keep it in a separate tub and mix with the vegetables when you are ready to eat them. You want a firm forkful, not a soggy mess!

Potatoes

Potatoes are found in the bread, other cereals and potatoes food group, but they are still a type of vegetable, and are really good for you.

Superspud

Potatoes are tubers and grow underground. They are one of nature's finest foods and are full of **carbohydrates**, fibre, vitamins and minerals. They provide energy and help to keep your body healthy and working in tip-top condition. They are also a good source of vitamin C, which helps to heal wounds – useful if you keep falling off your bike!

Keep your skin on

A lot of the goodness in potatoes is in the skin, so try to eat potatoes with the skin on whenever you can. This is why jacket, or baked, potatoes are a really healthy canteen lunch option, especially if they come with a tuna, cheese or bean filling and some other vegetables on the side.

Something different

For a delicious, easy and filling lunchbox dish, try potato salad. Eat it as a main meal or as a snack or side dish with some chicken, ham or tuna. Make the potato salad from boiled new potatoes with the skins on. Add sweetcorn, chopped red and green peppers, onion and peas for extra flavour. Stir it all together with some low-fat mayonnaise.

Little and large

There are loads of different types of potatoes. Big potatoes are perfect as jacket potatoes, and are even better with a tasty filling. Smaller varieties of potatoes are called new potatoes and are delicious when boiled and eaten with a little butter. You can even eat them cold the next day.

Chips

Yes, we know how good they taste and chips are fine as a weekly treat, but try not to eat them every day. Also, did you know that big, chunky chips have less fat than small 'French fry' style chips? So, if you are going to choose chips, go for the big 'uns!

CHECK IT OUT!

Try oven-baked chips or potato wedges. They are less fatty than fried chips and just as tasty.

15

Being a vegetarian

Many people are vegetarian for all sorts of reasons.

What is a vegetarian?

Being a vegetarian means you don't eat any meat or fish. Some people are also **vegan**. This means they don't eat any food that comes from an animal, such as eggs, milk or cheese. People become vegetarians for a variety of reasons: for their health, for their religious beliefs, because they don't like eating animals as food or because they just don't like the taste of meat. Being a vegetarian is very healthy as long as you make sure that you have a balanced diet.

Get balanced

If you don't eat meat, beans and pulses can provide some of the essential vitamins, minerals and protein that your body needs. You could have a bean salad for lunch and some cooked beans or lentils in the evening. There are loads of different types of beans, so experiment and see which you like best. As long as the beans are cooked properly, you can eat them hot in a stew or cold as part of a lunchtime salad.

VEGGIE LUNCHBOX SPECIAL

Try these options for a vegetarian packed lunch:

- Pitta bread pockets with houmous, avocado and tomato

- Brown rice salad with beans

- Leek and potato soup with added brown rice

- Mushroom salad in a tomato sauce

- Pasta salad with diced veggies

- Cold vegetable curry (Go on, give it a try. It tastes better than it sounds!)

- **Tortilla** wraps with beans, sweetcorn and lettuce

Lunch Choice

Three-bean salad

Have a bean feast for lunch. Mix 'n' match your favourite beans and add a few tasty extras for more flavour and goodness!

Banana

Bottle of milk

Beans means business

Beans are some of the best foods you can eat. They are bursting with protein, they taste really great and they fill you up! There's bound to be a bean to suit every taste. Choose from these beans for a perfect lunchtime munch.

Fruit salad

Borlotti beans

Cannellini or white beans

Black-eyed beans

Green beans

Get creative

Once you've chosen your beans, you can create some really great salads. Take your beans and add sweetcorn, chopped green and red peppers, peas, tuna, ham, diced chicken, sliced raw mushrooms, chopped tomato, leftover pasta... anything that takes your fancy! Add your favourite dressing, tub it up and tuck in at lunchtime.

Ready-made bean salad

CHECK IT OUT!

You can buy ready-made bean salads in different sauces. Give them a try, but check the label to see how much added salt and sugar they contain.

Three-bean salad

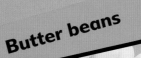

Butter beans

Red kidney beans

Bite Size

If you're using canned beans, drain and rinse them in cold water before adding them to your salad.

Salad bar

Salad vegetables are now available all year round, so there's no excuse not to have a healthy side dish in your lunchbox.

Weblink

For an exciting salad recipe, visit www.food.gov.uk/ healthiereating/ nutritionschools/bus /recipes/146407

Shake up your salad

Do you ever get bored of eating the same old things in a salad? Well, why not try mixing normal salad ingredients with some veggies that you might not usually add, for example, raw white cabbage, red cabbage, sliced red onions, sliced courgettes, cauliflower florets, beansprouts and fennel? They all taste fantastic and will transform your salad from sad... to super!

White cabbage

Fennel

Red cabbage

Red onions

Courgette

Cauliflower

Beansprouts

Cos lettuce

Rocket

Let us look at... lettuce!

Here are some of the different types of lettuce that you can buy in the shops and in the supermarket. Which ones have you tried?

Iceberg

Little gem

Lamb's leaf

Radicchio

Round lettuce

And there's more...

Now you've got the lettuce sorted, what else can you get at the salad bar?

Tomatoes

Spring onions

Cress

Radishes

Celery

Peppers

Beetroot

Cucumber

Get slicing and dicing for super salads at any time of the year!

Lunch Choice

Cool wraps

Enjoy your veggies ready wrapped. They're easy to eat and a tasty way to get some of your five portions of fruit and vegetables a day.

Yoghurt

Apple

Fajita fave

Slice your favourite vegetables into long sticks and wrap them up in a tortilla. This is a flat bread that comes from Mexico. Top with some salsa or avocado dip and roll up to make a **fajita**. Remember to fold in one end of your fajita or you'll end up with your lunch in your lap. What a waste that would be!

Pitta packet

Pack a tasty salad in a pitta pocket for a delicious lunch option. Spread some houmous inside a pitta and then fill it with cucumber, tomatoes and feta cheese. Yummy!

Bean big dipper

For a nutritious and delicious lunchbox snack, fill a flatbread or wrap with a selection of tasty beans and drizzle over your favourite dressing. Or, you could make a special bean big dipper. Mash up some beans, mix with low-fat mayonnaise and use a flatbread to scoop it up.

Bean big dipper

Fruit juice

Fajita wrap

Lettuce wrap things up

Experiment with making lettuce wraps. Spread your favourite dip on a large lettuce leaf, fill it with veggie sticks, roll up the lettuce leaf and munch away. Alternatively, try putting a sandwich filling, such as tuna mayonnaise, inside a lettuce leaf and rolling it up to make a parcel. You can make small, bite-sized lettuce parcels or larger parcels, but make sure you tuck the ends in before you eat!

Try five

You should try to eat at least five portions of fruit and vegetables a day, but what is a portion?

What a handful!

It's not as difficult as you think to eat at least five portions of fruit and vegetables a day. A portion is about the amount of raw veggies you can fit into the palm of your hand.

Weblink

Find out more about why eating five portions of veggies or fruit is good for you at www.5aday.nhs.uk You can get some great recipes and play some fab games, too!

A portion is also...

- A small can of vegetables

- A side salad

- The vegetables you get in a portion of vegetable curry, vegetable lasagne or vegetable casserole

- A medium-sized tomato

Fast food

Here are some ideas for making sure you eat your vegetables:

Veggie smoothie – blend celery, tomato juice and red peppers.

Vegetable pizza – top with a tomato sauce and red and green peppers.

Red gems – a handful of cherry tomatoes.

Cool kebabs – cubed veggies on a stick.

Veggie omelette – fill a thick omelette with peas, sweetcorn, onions and mushrooms, and eat cold for lunch.

A tub of beans – rinse and dry a can of mixed beans, put them in a tub or bag and pick at them for a snack.

Bite Size

For extra 'no hassle' veggies, add chopped, cooked vegetables to brown rice or a cold pasta salad.

Pinboard

Check out how vegetables are eaten in other countries...

Switzerland

Swiss potato cakes, called rosti, are like round, thick pancakes made from grated potato.

Russia

Borscht is a soup made from beetroot. It is eaten in Russia and is a reddish-purple colour.

Mexico

In Mexico, refried beans are used to make enchiladas. Corn tortillas are filled with a bean mix and cooked in the oven with a spicy sauce and melted cheese. 'Enchiladas' means 'cooked with chillies'.

Germany

Sauerkraut is cabbage that has been finely shredded and pickled. It comes from Germany and is often eaten with Frankfurter sausages.

Japan

In Japan, vegetable are dipped in a light batter and then fried to make vegetable tempura.

USA

Okra is added to a thick stew or soup called gumbo, which is made from rice and shellfish. Gumbo is common in the southern states of the USA.

Quiz time

Multiple-choice

1. Which of the following is not a vegetable?
a. pumpkin
b. tomato
c. celery
d. beetroot

2. Which of these vegetables are good for dipping?
a. red peppers
b. baby corn
c. pak choi
d. butternut squash

3. Which of the following is not a mushroom?
a. shiitake
b. sugarsnap
c. oyster
d. chanterelle

4. Which vegetables taste good both raw and cooked?
a. carrots
b. lettuce
c. broccoli
d. yellow peppers

5. What nutrients can be found in potatoes?
a. fibre
b. vitamin C
c. calcium
d. protein

Match the vegetable with its type

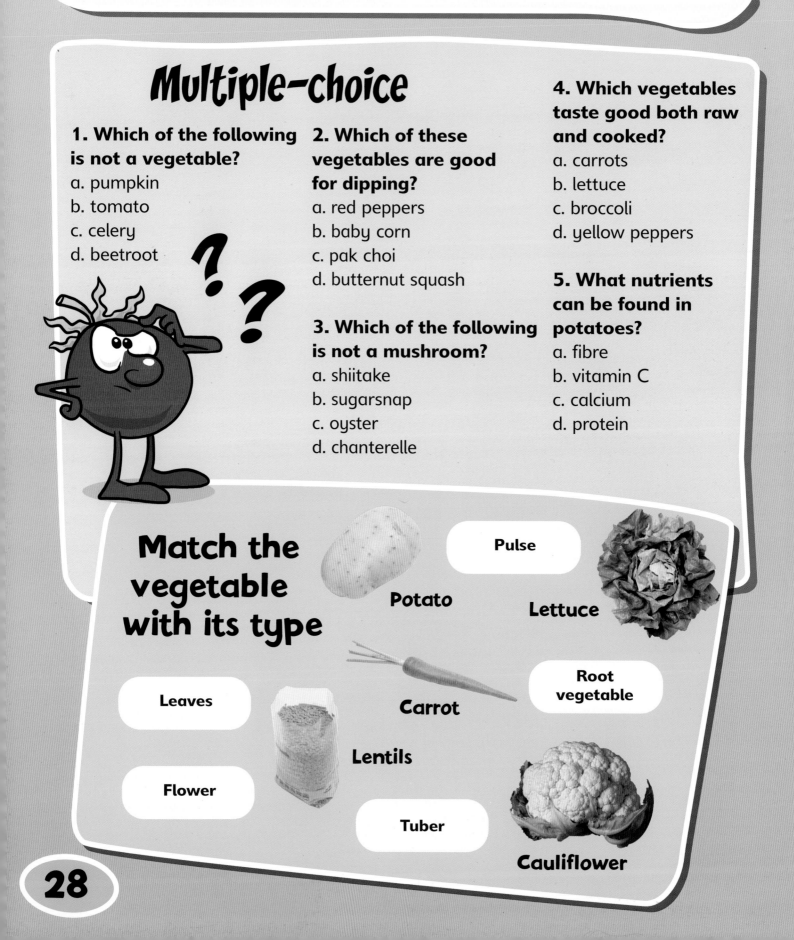

Pulse

Potato

Lettuce

Leaves

Carrot

Root vegetable

Lentils

Flower

Tuber

Cauliflower

28

True or false?

1. Potatoes are healthiest when fried.
2. Cold beetroot soup is called stew.
3. Vegetarians get protein from lettuce.
4. Red kidney beans are low in fat.
5. Radicchio is a type of lettuce.
6. Lettuce can be used for wraps.
7. Cherry tomatoes taste like cherries.
8. The Japanese dip vegetables in batter to make tempura.
9. Most vegetables are a good source of fibre.
10. Pulses are seeds from certain plants.

What's the answer?

1. What are the benefits of eating vegetables?
2. Why do we need vitamins?
3. Plan a vegetarian lunchbox menu for one week.
4. How many vegetables can you think of that can be eaten both raw and cooked?
5. Can you name a fruit or vegetable that starts with all the letters in your name?

Answers

True or false?
1. FALSE
2. FALSE
3. FALSE
4. TRUE
5. TRUE
6. TRUE
7. FALSE
8. TRUE
9. TRUE
10. TRUE

What's the answer?
There is not necessarily a right or a wrong answer to these questions, so discuss your answers with your teacher or a parent.

Multiple-choice
1. b – tomato
2. a and b – red peppers, baby corn
3. b – sugarsnap
4. a, c and d – carrots, broccoli, yellow peppers
5. a and b – fibre, vitamin C

Match the vegetable with its type
Carrot – Root vegetable
Lentils – Pulse
Potato – Tuber
Lettuce – Leaves
Cauliflower – Flower

Glossary

carbohydrate This is the part of the food you eat that gives your body energy

fajita A dish from Mexico that is made of meat or vegetables wrapped in a flat bread called a tortilla

fibre This is the part of food that helps your digestion work properly and makes sure you go to the toilet regularly

florets The parts of vegetables such as broccoli and cauliflower that are at the end of the stem and are good to eat

fungi A plant without leaves or flowers – such as mushrooms

Greek salad A salad made from tomatoes, onions, olives and cubes of feta cheese

horseradish This is a vegetable that is made into a hot paste or sauce. It tastes a bit like mustard

houmous Mashed chickpeas mixed with oil to make a dip or spread

minerals Substances found in certain foods which help to keep our bodies healthy, for example calcium, which helps strengthen bones and teeth

nutrients Substances such as vitamins and minerals that are found in the food we eat

portion A helping of one type of food to be eaten at one meal

protein Part of the food we eat which helps to build muscles and keep us healthy

pulses Seeds from plants that are used as a food, such as beans and lentils

salsa A tomato dip that is often spicy

tortilla A flat bread from Mexico

vegan A person who doesn't eat any meat, fish or other food that come from animals, such as milk, eggs or cheese (made from milk)

vegetarian A person who doesn't eat any meat or fish

vitamins Substances found in the food we eat which are essential to help us stay healthy. There are many different vitamins, such as A, B, C and D

Index

Parents' and teachers' notes

- Look at all the vegetables in the book. Have the children seen or heard of them before? Have they tasted these vegetables? Have they eaten them at home or somewhere else?

- Have a general talk about vegetables. What are the children's favourite vegetables? How do they like them cooked? Do they like raw vegetables?

- Build a picture chart of the children's favourite vegetables. Ask each child to bring a cut-out picture of the three vegetables they most like to eat. Stick the vegetables to the chart. Which are the top ten vegetables?

- Play 'Guess the Veg'. Draw a selection of vegetables from the book onto pieces of card. On the reverse, give three clues as to what the vegetable is. The children have to write down the name of the vegetable. Award points for the children who guess correctly. See who has the most points at the end of the game.

- Discuss a popular vegetable such as a potato. Talk about the different ways it can be eaten. Can it be eaten for breakfast, lunch and dinner? Can you take it on a picnic or have it in a school lunchbox?

- Discuss the different tastes of vegetables. Are some sweet? Do different vegetables taste better cooked or raw?

- Make a rainbow vegetable platter. Ask the children to draw a rainbow made up of vegetables that are the same colours as the rainbow.

- Make an alphabet chart of vegetables. Put a picture of a vegetable on the chart for each letter of the alphabet. Are there any letters without vegetables?